HOW TO LIVE A PURE LIFE THROUGH CHRIST

HOW TO LIVE A PURE LIFE THROUGH CHRIST

A Guide to Spiritual Transformation

LMD

CHAPTER 1: HIDDEN IN YOUR HEART

- Psalm 119:11 (NKJV) - "Your word I have hidden in my heart, That I might not sin against You."
- Exploring the importance of memorizing and internalizing Scripture to guard against impurity and sin.

CHAPTER 2: MEDITATION FOR TRANSFORMATION

- Psalm 119:12-13 (NKJV) - "Blessed are You, O Lord! Teach me Your statutes. With my lips, I have declared all the judgments of Your mouth."
- Delving into the transformative power of meditating on God's Word and declaring His truths in our lives.

CHAPTER 3: REJOICING IN THE WAY OF YOUR TESTIMONIES

- Psalm 119:14-16 (NKJV) - "I have rejoiced in the way of Your testimonies, As much as in all riches. I will meditate on Your precepts, And contemplate Your ways. I will delight myself in Your statutes; I will not forget Your word."
- Discussing the joy and richness found in living according to God's testimonies and finding delight in His statutes.

CHAPTER 4: THE COMFORTER WITHIN

- John 14:26 (NKJV) - "But the Helper, the Holy Spirit, whom the Father will send in My name, He will teach you all things, and bring to your remembrance all things that I said to you."

- Exploring the role of the Holy Spirit as the ultimate guide and teacher in our journey to live a pure life.

Chapter 5: God's Higher Ways

- Isaiah 55:9 (NKJV) - "For as the heavens are higher than the earth, So are My ways higher than your ways, And My thoughts than your thoughts."
- Understanding the significance of aligning our lives with God's higher ways to attain purity.

Chapter 6: Power, Love, and a Sound Mind

- 2 Timothy 1:7 (NKJV) - "For God has not given us a spirit of fear, but of power and of love and of a sound mind."
- Unpacking the concept that living a pure life is rooted in the power, love, and sound mind given by God, not in fear or impurity.

Chapter 7: Doers of the Word

- James 1:22 (NKJV) - "But be doers of the word, and not hearers only, deceiving yourselves."
- Emphasizing the importance of applying God's Word in our daily lives and the deception that comes with mere hearing without action.

Chapter 8: Purity of Thought and Intention

- Exploring the need for purity not only in actions but also in thoughts and intentions, aligning with the teachings of Psalm 119:11.

Chapter 9: Living in the Spirit

- Reflecting on the connection between living a pure life and walking in the Spirit, guided by the Helper mentioned in John 14:26.

Chapter 10: Transformed by Truth

- Summarizing the key principles and practices discussed in previous chapters and encouraging a commitment to a life transformed by God's truth for lasting purity.

PREFACE

Welcome to "How to Live a Pure Life: A Guide to Spiritual Transformation." In the journey of life, the pursuit of purity is a noble endeavor that transcends mere moral restraint; it is a transformative quest that touches the depths of the soul. This book is crafted with the intention of guiding you through ten essential chapters, each intricately woven with timeless wisdom drawn from sacred scriptures.

"Hidden in Your Heart" begins our exploration, urging you to anchor your life in the foundational truths of Psalm 119:11. As we delve into the significance of memorizing and internalizing God's Word, we pave the way for a resilient defense against the enticements of a world often marred by impurity.

Next, **"Meditation for Transformation"** invites you to discover the profound impact of meditating on the divine truths found in Psalm 119:12-13. Through this practice, we unlock the gateway to a life shaped by the principles of God's statutes and judgments.

"Rejoicing in the Way of Your Testimonies" expands on the joy and richness that arise from aligning our lives with God's testimonies, as expressed in Psalm 119:14-16. Delighting in His statutes becomes a source of strength, leading us away from forgetfulness and into a profound remembrance of His Word.

In **"The Comforter Within,"** we turn to the promise of John 14:26. The Holy Spirit, our Helper, takes center stage as the divine guide and teacher in our pursuit of purity, ensuring we are not left alone on this transformative journey.

"God's Higher Ways" challenges us to aspire to a life attuned to Isaiah 55:9, recognizing that God's ways are higher and holier than our own. This realization beckons us to elevate our standards and embrace a purer existence.

"Power, Love, and a Sound Mind" echoes the powerful words of 2 Timothy 1:7, affirming that living a pure life emanates from the divine gifts of power, love, and a sound mind—a stark departure from the bondage of fear and impurity.

"Doers of the Word" confronts the deception of a passive faith, drawing from the wisdom of James 1:22. Here, we emphasize the necessity of translating our understanding of God's Word into tangible action, making purity an active and lived reality.

As we progress, **"Purity of Thought and Intention"** compels us to explore the depths of our minds and intentions, aligning with the holistic purity advocated in Psalm 119:11.

"Living in the Spirit" probes the connection between purity and walking in the Spirit, in harmony with the teachings of John 14:26, inviting us to a life where the Holy Spirit is our constant guide.

Finally, in **"Transformed by Truth,"** we consolidate the insights from each chapter, urging you to commit to a life of lasting purity, transformed by the timeless truths encapsulated in this guide.

May this journey through the chapters inspire, challenge, and empower you to embark on the transformative path toward a life of enduring purity.

Chapter 1

"Hidden in Your Heart"

In the depths of our being, where the echoes of our thoughts and desires resonate, there exists a sacred space that cradles the very essence of who we are. It is in this intimate sanctum that we embark on our journey toward purity, guided by the profound wisdom encapsulated in Psalm 119:11— "Your word I have hidden in my heart, That I might not sin against You."

As we delve into the heart of this chapter, we are confronted with the transformative power of concealing God's Word within the recesses of our hearts. The act of memorizing and internalizing Scripture is not merely an intellectual exercise; rather, it is a deliberate and purposeful choice to safeguard our hearts against the pervasive allure of sin. In a world inundated with moral ambiguities and ethical compromises, the words we choose to hide within our hearts become a bulwark, a steadfast defense against the encroaching shadows of impurity.

The significance of Psalm 119:11 is illuminated as we explore the practical implications of this profound truth. Imagine a fortress, impervious to external threats, its walls fortified by the scriptures etched into the very fabric of its existence. Likewise, our hearts, when adorned with the Word of God, become resilient against the assaults of temptation and the subtle whispers of compromise. This intentional act of hiding God's Word is not an isolated event but a continuous process, a daily commitment to saturate our innermost being with the truths that emanate from the Creator Himself.

In the pursuit of purity, this chapter beckons us to cultivate a discipline of remembrance. It invites us to linger in the sacred verses that resonate with our spirits, letting them seep into the core of our identities. The memorization of Scripture is not a mere ritual but a deliberate shaping of our character—a conscious effort to align our hearts with the divine standard. In doing so, we equip ourselves with a reservoir of wisdom, a spiritual arsenal that empowers us to discern right from wrong and stand firm in the face of moral ambiguity.

As we embark on this exploration of hiding God's Word in our hearts, let us recognize it as an invitation to a transformative intimacy with the Divine. This chapter serves as a foundational cornerstone, urging us to embark on a journey where the Word of God becomes an indelible part of who we are, transforming our hearts into sanctuaries of purity.

CHAPTER 2

"MEDITATION FOR TRANSFORMATION"

In the quiet moments of contemplation, where the noise of the world fades away, we discover the profound impact of meditating on God's Word. Psalm 119:12-13 guides us on this transformative path, declaring, "Blessed are You, O Lord! Teach me Your statutes. With my lips, I have declared all the judgments of Your mouth." This chapter beckons us into the sacred space of meditation, where the timeless truths of Scripture become a wellspring of wisdom, shaping our perspectives and guiding our actions.

Meditation, in the context of this chapter, is not a passive activity but an intentional and purposeful engagement with the divine. It is an invitation to commune with the Creator, seeking His guidance and understanding through the study and reflection on His statutes. The word "blessed" echoes throughout these verses, emphasizing the inherent joy and fulfillment that accompany a life immersed in the meditation of God's precepts.

As we unravel the layers of meditation, we find it to be a dynamic process—an interplay between the written Word and our hearts. The psalmist's plea to be taught God's statutes is an acknowledgment of our need for divine guidance. This humility opens the door to a transformative exchange where the Creator imparts wisdom, and the seeker receives understanding. The act of declaring God's judgments with our lips is not a mere vocalization but a declaration of allegiance—a proclamation that the truths embedded in Scripture shape the very fabric of our identity.

The transformative power of meditation lies in its ability to transcend intellectual comprehension and seep into the core of our being. It is a journey from understanding to application—a movement from head knowledge to heart transformation. Through meditation, the scriptures cease to be distant words on a page; they become living and active, pulsating with relevance and application in our daily lives.

In the hustle and bustle of modern life, this chapter serves as a gentle reminder to carve out moments of stillness for meditation. It is an antidote to the cacophony of distractions that seek to drown out the voice of the Divine. As we immerse ourselves in the sacred practice of meditating on God's Word, we position ourselves for a transformation that transcends the superficial and touches the depths of our souls.

Let us embark on this chapter with an open heart and a willingness to be transformed. May the sacred act of meditation become a well-trodden path to spiritual growth, guiding us toward a life that reflects the blessedness of dwelling in the statutes of our Lord.

CHAPTER 3

"Rejoicing in the Way of Your Testimonies"

In the rhythm of life, amidst its myriad complexities and challenges, we find solace and joy in the testimonies of the Divine. Psalm 119:14-16 resonates with a melody of rejoicing, declaring, "I have rejoiced in the way of Your testimonies, As much as in all riches. I will meditate on Your precepts, And contemplate Your ways. I will delight myself in Your statutes; I will not forget Your word." This chapter invites us into a celebration of God's testimonies, a source of joy that surpasses worldly riches and endures beyond fleeting pleasures.

The psalmist's exuberance is palpable as they express not just a passive acknowledgment but an active rejoicing in the way of God's testimonies. This rejoicing is not confined to moments of ease but extends into the very fabric of our lives, woven into the tapestry of our daily experiences. It is a rejoicing that transcends circumstances, finding its source in the unchanging and eternal nature of God's Word.

The chapter encourages us to engage in a multi-faceted exploration: to meditate on God's precepts, to contemplate His ways, and to delight in His statutes. These actions are not isolated endeavors but interconnected components of a holistic relationship with the Divine. Meditation opens the door to understanding, contemplation deepens our insight, and delighting in God's statutes fosters a joy that becomes our strength.

The comparison of this joy to riches is striking—a deliberate choice to juxtapose the fleeting allure of material wealth with the enduring richness found in God's testimonies. The wealth of the world may provide temporary gratification, but the joy derived from the testimonies of the Divine is a wellspring that never runs dry. It is a wealth that transcends the limitations of the temporal and extends into the eternal.

As we navigate the intricacies of this chapter, we are reminded of the importance of intentional remembrance. The commitment to not forget God's Word is an anchor that grounds us in the midst of life's storms. It is a deliberate choice to carry the testimonies of the Divine in our hearts, allowing them to shape our perspectives, guide our decisions, and infuse our lives with a joy that surpasses understanding.

This chapter calls us to a life of celebration—a jubilation that arises from the deep wellsprings of our souls. It is an invitation to not only acknowledge but actively rejoice in the way of God's testimonies, finding in them a source of enduring joy that sustains us through the various seasons of life. May our hearts resonate with the psalmist's declaration as we embark on a journey of rejoicing in the profound and life-giving testimonies of the Divine.

CHAPTER 4

"THE COMFORTER WITHIN"

In the labyrinth of life's journey, where challenges and uncertainties abound, we find solace in the promise of divine guidance. John 14:26 unveils this comforting assurance, declaring, "But the Helper, the Holy Spirit, whom the Father will send in My name, He will teach you all things, and bring to your remembrance all things that I said to you." This chapter is an exploration of the profound role of the Holy Spirit as the Comforter within, a divine presence that illuminates our path and imparts wisdom for the journey.

The opening words, "But the Helper," serve as a beacon of hope amid life's complexities. In a world often marked by uncertainty and challenges, the promise of a Helper, a divine companion, is an anchor that grounds us. The Holy Spirit is not merely a passive observer but an active participant in our lives—a Helper who comes alongside to navigate the twists and turns of our spiritual journey.

As we delve into the chapter, the imagery of the Holy Spirit as a Teacher emerges. "He will teach you all things" resonates as an invitation to a continuous and transformative learning experience. The Holy Spirit, as the ultimate Guide and Instructor, imparts not only knowledge but also a deeper understanding of the truths

7

embedded in the teachings of Christ. This divine instruction transcends the limits of human intellect, reaching into the realms of the heart and spirit.

The aspect of remembrance is a poignant theme in this chapter. "And bring to your remembrance all things that I said to you" signifies the Holy Spirit's role in reinforcing the teachings of Christ within us. In the ebb and flow of life, where distractions abound and memories falter, the Comforter within ensures that the timeless truths of Christ are etched into the fabric of our being. It is a divine assurance that we are not left to navigate the complexities of life's decisions and dilemmas alone.

This chapter prompts us to cultivate a sensitivity to the Holy Spirit's guidance, to attune our hearts to the whispers of divine wisdom. It invites us to embrace the transformative power of the Comforter within, recognizing that the Helper is not a distant force but a personal and intimate presence in our lives. The Holy Spirit becomes the lens through which we perceive the world, the gentle nudging that steers us away from pitfalls and towards the path of righteousness.

As we embark on this exploration of the Comforter within, may our hearts be open to the divine guidance and instruction that the Holy Spirit offers. May we find comfort in the assurance that we are not alone, for the Helper, the Holy Spirit, is within, teaching, guiding, and bringing to remembrance the profound truths that sustain us on our spiritual journey.

CHAPTER 5

"GOD'S HIGHER WAYS"

In the tapestry of our existence, woven with threads of joy and challenges, we are beckoned to align our lives with the higher ways of the Divine. Isaiah 55:9 unfolds this invitation with resounding clarity, proclaiming, "For as the heavens are higher than the earth, So are My ways higher than your ways, And My thoughts than your thoughts." This chapter is an odyssey into the profound concept of God's higher ways, urging us to transcend our limited perspectives and embrace the majestic wisdom inherent in the divine plan.

The analogy presented in Isaiah 55:9 invites us to contemplate the vast expanse that separates the heavens from the earth. It is a visual representation of the immeasurable distance between our finite understanding and the boundless wisdom of the Creator. The inherent contrast challenges us to release the constraints of our human reasoning and acknowledge the sovereignty of God's ways—an acknowledgment that lays the foundation for a transformative journey.

God's higher ways, as explored in this chapter, transcend the realm of human comprehension. They represent a divine blueprint that, when embraced, elevates our existence beyond the mundane and temporal. To align with God's higher ways is to surrender the illusion of control and yield to the guidance of a Creator whose thoughts surpass our understanding. It is an acknowledgment that our perspectives are inherently limited, and in recognizing this limitation, we open ourselves to the infinite possibilities embedded in God's higher ways.

As we navigate the depths of this chapter, the call to align with God's higher ways becomes an invitation to transcend the limitations of our own understanding. It is a beckoning to release the grip of self-reliance and walk in humble submission to the divine order. The pursuit of God's higher ways is not a quest for blind obedience but an expedition into the heart of a Creator whose wisdom surpasses our own—a wisdom that unfolds in the tapestry of our lives with divine precision.

This chapter prompts us to reflect on our own inclinations and biases, challenging us to discern where our ways diverge from God's higher ways. It invites us to lay aside the pride that often accompanies human reasoning and embrace the humility required to walk in step with the divine. The journey into God's higher ways is an ongoing process of transformation—a commitment to continually seek, trust, and align with the majestic wisdom that transcends our understanding.

May this chapter be a compass guiding us toward a life attuned to God's higher ways, where the heavens touch the earth, and the divine wisdom shapes the course of our journey. As we embark on this exploration, may we find solace in surrender, wisdom in humility, and purpose in aligning our lives with the higher ways of the Creator.

Chapter 6

"Power, Love, and a Sound Mind"

In the intricate tapestry of our humanity, we are endowed with divine gifts—power, love, and a sound mind. These gifts, as unveiled in 2 Timothy 1:7, echo with profound significance, declaring, "For God has not given us a spirit of fear, but of power and of love and of a sound mind." This chapter delves into the transformative implications of this empowering verse, guiding us toward a life characterized by courage, compassion, and clarity of thought.

The contrast drawn in the opening words of the verse is stark and purposeful. The spirit of fear, often an unwelcome companion in the human experience, is replaced by a triumvirate of divine endowments—power, love, and a sound mind. These gifts, bestowed by a benevolent Creator, redefine the contours of our existence, inviting us to step into a reality where fear holds no dominion.

The exploration of power in this chapter extends beyond mere physical might. It is a power rooted in spiritual resilience, an internal fortitude that enables us to confront challenges with unwavering confidence. It is the power to overcome adversity, to persevere in the face of uncertainty, and to walk in the assurance of divine strength. As we absorb the implications of this divine empowerment, it becomes a catalyst for a life free from the paralyzing grip of fear.

Love emerges as the second facet of our divine endowment, and its significance cannot be overstated. It is a transformative force that redirects our focus from self-centered fear to others-oriented compassion. This love is not limited to sentimental expressions but extends to selfless actions, shaping relationships, and fostering a sense of interconnectedness. In a world often marked by division, the infusion of divine love becomes a counter-cultural force that transcends boundaries and unifies hearts.

The third element, a sound mind, signifies a mental clarity and discernment that emanates from the divine source. It is an antidote to the confusion and chaos that often permeate human thinking. This sound mind enables us to navigate the complexities of life with wisdom, making decisions that align with God's purposes. As we embrace this gift, our thought processes are anchored in truth, contributing to a life characterized by coherence and purpose.

This chapter serves as an invitation to examine our lives in the light of 2 Timothy 1:7. It prompts us to identify areas where fear may be exerting undue influence and challenges us to exchange that fear for the divine endowments of power, love, and a sound mind. As we navigate the complexities of our existence, may this chapter be a guide, steering us toward a life marked by courage, compassion, and clarity—a life that reflects the divine imprint of our Creator.

CHAPTER 7

"DOERS OF THE WORD"

In the symphony of faith, the call to action reverberates with unwavering clarity. James 1:22 conducts this call with precision, declaring, "But be doers of the word, and not hearers only, deceiving yourselves." This chapter unravels the profound implications of this directive, inviting us to move beyond passive reception and into the transformative realm of actively embodying the truths found in the Word of God.

The verse begins with a poignant contrast between hearing and doing, emphasizing the inherent danger of self-deception when one remains a mere hearer. The call to be doers of the word is not a suggestion; it is a clarion call to authentic discipleship—a summons to translate belief into action. The deceptive allure of merely hearing without doing is exposed, and in its place emerges an imperative to embody the teachings of Scripture in tangible, real-world expressions.

The chapter prompts a reflective examination of our own lives. Are we content with a passive reception of God's Word, letting it wash over us without effecting change? Or are we willing to be transformed into active participants in the divine narrative, living out the principles and precepts we claim to believe? The call to be doers beckons us to bridge the gap between belief and action, dismantling the illusion of a faith confined to words alone.

To be a doer of the word is to engage in a dynamic dance of faith—a partnership with the divine where obedience becomes the rhythm and action becomes the choreography. It is an acknowledgment that faith, when lived out, is a force that extends beyond the confines of religious rituals and permeates every facet of our lives. This chapter encourages us to view the Word of God not as a passive script but as an active guide, shaping our decisions, influencing our interactions, and directing the course of our journey.

As we navigate the depths of this chapter, it compels us to confront the potential hypocrisy that arises when our actions do not align with our professed beliefs. It challenges us to cultivate an authenticity that transcends the superficial, inviting us to embody the transformative power of God's Word in our daily lives. The call to be doers of the word is an invitation to a life where our faith is not a static creed but a dynamic force that impacts the world around us.

May this chapter serve as a catalyst for a faith that moves beyond mere rhetoric, a faith that is expressed in actions, and a faith that reflects the transformative power of a living, active relationship with the Word of God. As we embark on the journey of being doers, may our lives resonate with the harmony of a faith lived out in vibrant and authentic ways.

"Purity of Thought and Intention"

In the sanctum of our minds, the seeds of our actions are sown. This truth is illuminated in the exploration of Chapter 8, centered around the imperative for purity of thought and intention. Building upon the foundational principles of Psalm 119:11, this chapter challenges us to cultivate a purity that transcends external actions, reaching into the very core of our being.

Psalm 119:11 reminds us of the significance of hiding God's Word in our hearts as a guard against sin. This chapter takes us a step further, urging us to extend this guardianship to the realm of our thoughts and intentions. Purity of thought is not a mere ideal; it is a transformative discipline that demands vigilance and intentionality. The chapter prompts us to examine the motives behind our thoughts, recognizing that the state of our hearts shapes the trajectory of our actions.

In a world where external appearances often take precedence, the call to purity of intention challenges us to go beyond the surface. It invites us to scrutinize our motives, questioning whether our actions are driven by self-interest, societal expectations, or a genuine desire to align with God's standards. The chapter is a mirror that reflects the purity—or lack thereof—residing within the chambers of our minds.

As we navigate the depth of this chapter, it becomes evident that purity of thought and intention is not a legalistic checklist but a relational pursuit. It is about aligning our innermost desires with the character of God, allowing the transformative power of His Word to permeate every facet of our thinking. The call to purity is an invitation to surrender the broken fragments of our intentions to the mending touch of divine grace.

This chapter prompts self-reflection—an exploration of the motives that underpin our thoughts and actions. It challenges us to recognize and confront the subtle influences that can taint our intentions. Through this introspection, we discover that purity is not a destination but a continual journey—a journey that requires humility, vulnerability, and a commitment to allow God's refining fire to purify the motives of our hearts.

The journey to purity of thought and intention is not a solitary endeavor. It is a partnership with the Holy Spirit, the divine Helper whose transformative presence guides us toward a state of inner purity. As we embark on this chapter, may our hearts be open to the sanctifying work of the Spirit, and may our thoughts and intentions align with the purity found in the timeless truths of God's Word. May the pursuit of purity be a testament to the transformative power of a mind and heart renewed by the grace of the Divine.

CHAPTER 9

"LIVING IN THE SPIRIT"

In the tapestry of our spiritual journey, the invitation to "live in the Spirit" stands as a profound directive, echoing the transformative promise of divine guidance and empowerment. Rooted in the teachings of John 14:26, this chapter delves into the significance of aligning our lives with the Spirit—a beckoning to relinquish self-reliance and embark on a journey where the divine presence becomes our constant guide.

John 14:26 introduces the Holy Spirit as the Helper sent by the Father in Jesus' name. This chapter unfolds the rich implications of living in the Spirit—an existence characterized by a dynamic partnership with the divine. To live in the Spirit is to embrace a life where the Holy Spirit is not a distant force but an intimate companion, a guiding presence that influences our thoughts, decisions, and actions.

The transformative nature of living in the Spirit is illuminated through the lens of divine guidance. The Holy Spirit, as the Helper, assumes the role of a constant companion on our journey. This divine guidance is not limited to moments of crisis but extends into the nuances of our daily existence. It is a guidance that shapes our perspectives, providing clarity in moments of uncertainty and directing our steps along the path of right-eousness.

Living in the Spirit also encompasses the concept of surrender —a willingness to yield to the divine influence and trust in the unfolding of God's plan. The Spirit becomes a source of empowerment, equipping us with the strength to overcome challenges and the resilience to navigate the complexities of life. The chapter invites us to release the grip of self-reliance and embrace a life where the Spirit becomes the driving force behind our actions.

As we navigate the depth of this chapter, it prompts us to evaluate the posture of our hearts. Are we living in the Spirit, allowing the divine presence to permeate every facet of our existence? Or are we resisting the transformative work of the Helper, relying solely on our own understanding and strength? The call to live in the Spirit is a call to surrender, an invitation to align our lives with the divine current that flows in harmony with God's purposes.

The chapter concludes with a recognition that living in the Spirit is not a solitary endeavor but a communal experience. As individuals living in the Spirit, we become part of a larger community, connected by a shared journey of transformation. The Spirit unifies believers, creating a spiritual synergy that transcends individual efforts and fosters a collective pursuit of righteousness.

May this chapter inspire a deepening awareness of the Holy Spirit's presence in our lives. May it lead us into a transformative journey where living in the Spirit becomes a guiding principle— an existence marked by divine guidance, empowered surrender, and a communal pursuit of righteousness. As we embark on this exploration, may our lives be a testament to the transformative power of living in the Spirit.

CHAPTER 10

CONCLUSION: "TRANSFORMED BY TRUTH"

As we draw the final curtains on our exploration through the chapters, culminating in the transformative essence of "Transformed by Truth," we find ourselves at the nexus of profound revelation and practical application. Each chapter has been a stepping stone in a journey towards purity, wisdom, and alignment with the divine. Now, we stand at the threshold, poised to embrace the culmination of these insights in a life wholly transformed by the timeless truths encapsulated in the Word of God.

Chapter 10, "Transformed by Truth," serves as the capstone—a rallying call to consolidate the principles and practices garnered from the preceding chapters. Here, the spotlight shines on the transformative power embedded in God's truth. The Word of God is not a mere compilation of ancient wisdom but a living, breathing force capable of shaping our thoughts, actions, and very identities. To be transformed by truth is to allow the divine revelation to penetrate the recesses of our hearts, catalyzing a metamorphosis that transcends the superficial and permeates the essence of our being.

The transformative power of truth is not a theoretical proposition but a lived reality. It beckons us to embrace the Word of

God not as an abstract concept but as a dynamic force that guides our decisions, influences our relationships, and propels us along the path of righteousness. The truths encapsulated in Scripture are not confined to the pages of a book; they are catalysts for personal and societal change—a force that, when embraced, has the capacity to impact the world around us.

As we reflect on the journey undertaken through the chapters, we recognize that transformation is not a one-time event but a continual process—a dynamic interplay between revelation and response. Each chapter, from "Hidden in Your Heart" to "Living in the Spirit," has contributed a unique facet to the mosaic of transformation. From the discipline of memorization to the surrender of living in the Spirit, the chapters have guided us through a multifaceted exploration of what it means to live a life aligned with divine principles.

The call to be "doers of the word" resonates through each chapter, challenging us to move beyond passive reception and into the realm of active discipleship. Purity, wisdom, and alignment with God's higher ways are not abstract ideals but lived realities— an embodiment of the transformative power of truth in our lives.

In conclusion, our journey has been an odyssey of discovery— a discovery of the richness inherent in God's testimonies, the comfort provided by the Holy Spirit, the wisdom found in God's higher ways, the empowerment of divine gifts, the purity of thought and intention, and the transformative journey of living in the Spirit. Now, we stand at the precipice of transformation, the culmination of our journey. "Transformed by Truth" is not just a chapter; it is a paradigm shift—a declaration that we are not defined by our past or limited by our circumstances, but rather, we are continually being shaped by the timeless truths that emanate from the heart of the Divine.

As we step forward from this culmination, may our lives be a living testament to the transformative power of God's truth. May we be vessels through which the wisdom, purity, and empowerment gained from our exploration flow into the world around us.

The journey does not end here; it extends into the vast expanse of our future, where each step is guided by the transformative truth we've unearthed along this sacred odyssey. May we be forever transformed by the enduring, life-giving truth encapsulated in the Word of God.

www.ingramcontent.com/pod-product-compliance
Lightning Source LLC
Chambersburg PA
CBHW071300130726
47998CB00003B/1272